a١١ ᴏᴀ
١299
30/9

DECIMUS ⌐

Architect ɑ

(1800

Dr Philip Whitbourn OBE

Royal Tunbridge Wells Civic Society
Local History Monograph No.1

Published by
The Royal Tunbridge Wells Civic Society
2003

Published in Great Britain in 2003 by
The Local History Group of
The Royal Tunbridge Wells Civic Society

All rights reserved.

No part of this publication may be reproduced,
stored in a retrieval system, or transmitted,
in any form or by any means,
without the prior permission of the copyright holder.
Within the UK, exceptions are allowed
in respect of any 'fair dealing' for the purpose of
research or private study, or criticism or review,
as permitted under
the Copyright, Designs and Patents Act, 1988

© Royal Tunbridge Wells Civic Society

Dr. Philip Whitbourn has asserted his right
to be identified as the author of this work
in accordance with
the Copyright, Designs and Patents Act, 1988

ISBN No. 0 9545343 0 1

The text is set in Bookman Old Style 10 pt.
and the front cover in Bookman Old Style 16pt.

Front cover: The Victoria entrance arch to Calverley Park,
Tunbridge Wells, designed by Decimus Burton.

Printed and bound by The Ink Pot Lithographic Printers,
Southborough, Tunbridge Wells, Kent TN4 0LT

CONTENTS

Trinity Church, Church Road, Tunbridge Wells, designed by Decimus Burton and
exhibited at the Royal Academy in 1827. Declared pastorally redundant by the
church authorities in 1972 and re-opened as Trinity Arts Centre in 1982.

ACKNOWLEDGEMENTS

In 1981 Philip Miller, at that time an active member of the Royal Tunbridge Wells Civic Society, and I co-operated over the staging of an exhibition to mark the centenary of Decimus Burton's death in 1881. This exhibition was in two parts, the first comprising Philip Miller's panels from a display held at the Building Centre in London, which focused upon the national picture. These were shown in the emerging Trinity Arts Centre. The second part was a collection of local material assembled jointly with Tunbridge Wells Museum and this was shown in the Municipal Art Gallery. Philip Miller's catalogue for the Building Centre display has remained for more than twenty years the most useful and authoritative work on Decimus Burton, and it includes a list of all Burton's works known at that time. Other such lists are to be found in "The Builder" obituary and in Howard Colvin's Biographical Dictionary of British Architects, a standard work on the subject of architectural history. My wish has been to try to complement Philip Miller's work as far as possible, rather than simply to duplicate it.

In preparing this monograph, I am grateful for the help of colleagues in the Civic Society and, especially to the Committee of its Local History Group: Secretary, John Cunningham; Tunbridge Wells Museum's Local History Officer, Dr Ian Beavis; Tunbridge Wells Reference Team Librarian, Sue Brown; and Tunbridge Wells historian Roger Farthing: and particularly to Mary Woodruffe, a member of the Civic Society and Local History Group, who struggled valiantly and with *complete* success to turn my manuscript into such perfect typescript.

I acknowledge too, the help of staff at the Centre for Kentish Studies, the Victoria and Albert Museum, the RIBA Drawings Collection, the Zoological Society of London, the Royal Botanic Gardens at Kew, the Royal Academy of Arts, the Society of Antiquaries of London, the Public Record Office, Tunbridge Wells Library, Bromley Central Library, Southborough Library, Tunbridge Wells Museum, Hastings Museum, Tonbridge School and several individuals including Peter Miall, John Fuller, Frieda Hansard, John Kennedy, the Revd.W.H. Simpson, and Gill and Roger Joye.

Philip Whitbourn,
Tunbridge Wells 2003

Greek Doric columns in Decimus Burton's Calverley Market, Tunbridge Wells, later the Old Town Hall. Regrettably demolished in December 1959.

INTRODUCTION

"Decimus Burton Esq., Architect and Gentleman, well versed in the History and Antiquities of this Kingdom." So read a testimonial in 1828, recommending Burton for election to Fellowship of the Society of Antiquaries of London (1).

A meeting of the Society of Antiquaries in Somerset House in the 1830s

The election duly took place on 8th January 1829 and it was doubly appropriate that the Society's Vice President, W.R. Hamilton, was in the chair on that particular occasion. In the first place, Hamilton was Chief Commissioner of Woods and Forests, the government office that had commissioned Burton to undertake his well-received improvements to Hyde Park. Then, secondly, Hamilton, sometime Secretary to Lord Elgin, had superintended the safe transportation to England of the famous Grecian marbles in 1802. Between 1806 and 1812 the sculptures were being assembled and they were bought for the nation in 1817. That was the year in which young Decimus embarked upon his architectural career and, by then, the "Greek Revival" had become firmly established.

During the course of Burton's long time in professional practice, the once fashionable Greek Revival fell out of favour. Nevertheless, before his death in 1881 the serious Gothic Revival that replaced the Grecian taste was faltering too, as his last pupil E.J. May took over from Norman Shaw as Estate Architect for the "Queen Anne" style "Garden Suburb" of Bedford Park in London. For the perfect "prototype garden suburb" however, one need look no further than the Calverley New Town in Tunbridge Wells, where the neo-classical, and Old English and Gothick villas in the picturesque setting of Calverley Park constitute "a landmark in English domestic architecture" (2).

Decimus Burton Esq., FRS, FSA

Calverley Park, Tunbridge Wells

CHAPTER 1

INFLUENCES AT WORK

So far as is known, Decimus Burton left no autobiography, diaries or treatises expounding his architectural philosophy. So any insights into his thoughts about architecture have to be gleaned from his works themselves and from such knowledge as exists about his life and times.

As his name suggests, Decimus was the tenth child of the successful architect and builder James Burton (1761-1837), alias Haliburton, and his wife Elizabeth. Originally of Scottish stock, James was descended from John Haliburton (1573-1627) from whom Sir Walter Scott could also trace his descent. The first four of the Burton children were christened using the former surname Haliburton, but, after that, the name was shortened to Burton.

Of the twelve siblings, William, Emma (died young), Eliza, James, Emily (died young), Jane, Septimus, Octavia, Henry, Decimus, Alfred and Jessy, only Decimus followed seriously in his father's architectural footsteps. James showed early signs of doing so and worked with the well-known architect Sir John Soane for a while but, in the event, became a noted Egyptologist. Alfred, too, had some architectural background and worked with his brother Decimus at one stage, but was involved for much of his life with family property and public duties at St.Leonards. Septimus started as a lawyer with much of his father's business, while Henry, a former pupil at Tonbridge School, became a Professor at St.Thomas's Hospital (1).

Mabledon, Quarry Hill c.1810

Decimus was born in London on 30th September 1800, and it was after Jessy's arrival four years later that the Burtons moved the family home out of London to a country seat at Quarry Hill on the rural outskirts of Southborough.

Thus Decimus's childhood and formative years were spent among the traceried gothic windows and battlements of the castellated mansion called Mabledon, and the varied scenery of its considerable grounds (2).

In 1816 Decimus entered his father's office, where he received good practical experience, supplemented by training under the architect and drawing-master George Maddox (1760-1843). In around 1819 or 1820 Maddox made for Decimus Burton a ten-leaved album of sketches, which Burton presented to the Royal Institute of British Architects in 1869. The sketches were described by Wyatt Papworth, sometime Curator of Sir John Soane's Museum, as "wonderful specimens of handwork" and as showing "great originality of design" (3).

One of the leaves of the album of sketches made for Decimus Burton by the architect George Maddox in about 1820. (Courtesy: RIBA Library Drawings Collection.)

10

On 14th November 1817 Decimus Burton entered the Royal Academy Schools at the age of 17. Then situated in Somerset House, the Royal Academy was established in 1768 and its Instrument of Foundation provided, among other things, that there shall be a Professor of Architecture. The Professor of Architecture had a duty to read annually six public lectures, "calculated to form the taste of students, to instruct them in the laws and principles of composition, to point out to them the beauties or faults of celebrated productions, to fit them for an unprejudiced study of books, and for critical examination of structures" (4).

Sir John Soane was Professor of Architecture from 1806 until his death in 1837. Soane delivered regular and substantial lectures from 1809 onwards, illustrating them with large drawings specially prepared by his pupils and assistants, although there were no lectures in 1814 or 1816, when Soane's wife was ill and died, nor in 1818.

In 1817, Soane remodelled his lectures, making them more discursive about forms of classical architecture, and in 1819 his lectures numbered I to VI were given, followed by lectures VII to IX in 1820. In lecture VI Soane observed that in many buildings of that time, roofs and chimney shafts were not considered to be of as much compositional importance as they had been in former periods. Soane went on: "To treat a roof merely as a protection from the weather, and the chimney shaft only as a tube to convey away the smoke, is not sufficient. These parts", he added, "are decidedly of great value in the general effect of a building........" (5). In lecture VII Soane comments upon aspects of villa design, making the point that architectural character should be determined by the surrounding scenery (6).

Other contemporary students at the Royal Academy Schools included the 19 year-old Sidney Smirke, also on the 1817 intake, and the 20 year-old William Tite (later Sir William) in 1818. Burton's friend Sidney Smirke was later to co-operate with him over the restoration of the Temple Church in London and to become a resident of Tunbridge Wells.

Some of the casts from Decimus Burton's collection in the Victoria and Albert Museum. *Top:* Moulding with floral ornament, after a Roman original. *Centre left:* Pair of brackets with acanthus, after original in the Vatican; egg and dart moulding, after a Roman original. *Centre right:* Guilloche on a pilaster, after a Roman original. *Bottom:* Ionic capital, after an original in S. Maria in Trastevere, Rome

Like Soane, Burton had a large collection of casts of ornament that informed his work, more than two hundred of which were given to the

Victoria and Albert Museum. Eighteen of these were selected for display in the British Galleries (7).

High on any list of influences on young Decimus must, of course, be those of his father, James, and his father's friend, John Nash (1752-1835), Architect to King George IV. Although best known for his great classical works such as Chester Terrace in Regent's Park, Nash was, at one time, in partnership with the leading landscape designer Humphrey Repton (1752-1818), and he was responsible for picturesque works too, such as the famous Blaise Hamlet near Bristol. Indeed, it was often expected of architects of the Regency period that they would be able to work in more than one style when necessary. Thus, other major architects of the era, such as Sir Robert Smirke and William Wilkins worked, like Nash, Burton and even Soane, in more than one architectural idiom, depending upon the particular circumstances.

The early 19th century was a period of great change. Throughout Decimus Burton's boyhood Britain was at war with France, and the Battle of Waterloo was fought in 1815, the year before the youthful Decimus entered his father's office. Although the return of peace brought unemployment among the poor, post Waterloo was also an era of church building and Gentlemen's Clubs. Want of labour during the war had given impetus to the industrial revolution and, had more of Burton's British Ironworks of 1826-7 survived at Abersychan, South Wales (8), they would have been of the greatest interest as industrial monuments.

Iron was an important element in many Burton buildings, ranging from the Neo-Classical Wellington Arch and Charing Cross Hospital to the great stoves at Chatsworth and Kew.

Burton's earlier works predate the coming of the railways, but it was through the procuring of an Act of Parliament by 1835 that the Preston and Wyre Railway Company was born (9), and Burton's new town of Fleetwood created.

It is known that Burton travelled to Venice and elsewhere on the continent (10), and that he toured Canada and the United States in the company of Judge Haliburton, starting from Liverpool to Halifax, Nova Scotia, on the "Arabia" (11).

CHAPTER 2

CLIENTS AND CONNECTIONS

No architect can practise his or her profession in any practical way without some form of client or patron. For the first commission of a budding young architect to come from a member of the family may not be unusual, but a brief to an eighteen year old for a lakeside villa in London's Regent's Park was a remarkable circumstance indeed.

Decimus Burton's father, James, had leased the land in 1815 and by 1818 the family was in occupation at "The Holme" in Regent's Park (1). The central feature of the garden front was a projecting bow, an arrangement that Burton was to use elsewhere later on, including at nos. 7 and 15 Calverley Park, Tunbridge Wells.

The Holme, Regent's Park, c.1827.

The Holme was followed in 1818-19 by South Villa, Regent's Park, for David Lance (sadly, demolished in 1930), by Cornwall and Clarence Terraces in Regent's Park in 1821 and 1823, and in 1822-24 by Grove House, Regent's Park, for George Bellas Greenough. This latter building still survives as Nuffield Lodge.

Cornwall Terrace, Regent's Park in 1827

George Greenough (1778-1855), an eminent geographer and geologist, had inherited a fortune from his maternal grandfather, and it was through Greenough that Burton was commissioned to design the Athenaeum Club in London (2), an institution of which he was an early member, and through which he was to meet further of his clients. Greenough, along with Sir Humphrey Davy, was also a member of the Council of the Zoological Society of London, Burton's clients for London Zoo.

The Athenaeum Building Committee, Burton's clients for the Athenaeum Club building, consisted of the Earl of Aberdeen, sometime Prime Minister and President of the Society of Antiquaries; Sir Thomas Lawrence, President of the Royal Academy; Sir Humphrey Davy, President of the Royal Society and inventor of the famous safety lamp; Sir Robert Smirke, RA, FRS, FSA, Architect of the British Museum; John Wilson Croker, MP; Joseph Jekyll, KC, FRS, MP; Richard Heber, DCL, MP; and Charles Hatchett, FRS; the first three being the trustees of the Club (3).

That Burton continued as architect to the Club until 1864, some forty years after being approached, must be an indication of his professional ability in dealing with such an illustrious client body. It was significant too that John Wilson Croker, the visionary behind the inception of the Athenaeum Club in 1823, had Decimus Burton as

15

architect for his marine villa at Stokes Bay, near Gosport, in around 1840.

The client, in 1827, for Decimus Burton's fourth villa in Regent's Park, Hanover Lodge, was Lt.General Sir Robert Arbuthnot, KCB. Sir Robert had seen action in the Peninsular War and had been at the battle of Corunna. He was the brother of Charles Arbuthnot, the diplomat and politician who presided over the government's Office of Woods and Forests.

Charles Arbuthnot was one of that group of "five or six noblemen and gentlemen" from whom Decimus Burton took instructions for work at Hyde Park Corner in London. That group was no less distinguished than the Building Committee for the Athenaeum and comprised: Lord Liverpool, the Prime Minister; Lord Goderich, the Chancellor of the Exchequer; Sir Robert Peel, at that time Home Secretary, but later Prime Minister; J.C. Herries, Financial Secretary to the Treasury; and Lord Farnborough, FRS, FSA, a former Paymaster General and respected judge of art and architecture (4).

A complete list of noblemen and gentlemen from whom Decimus Burton took instructions professionally during the course of his long career as an architect would be lengthy. It would feature at least a dozen members of the House of Lords, including two Dukes, two Marquesses, and two Earls, at least a further couple of dozen assorted Baronets, Knights, Members of Parliament and Clergy, and numbers of Esquires and Gentlemen.

One important Baronet was Sir David Salomons, for whom Burton designed Burrswood in Groombridge, and Broomhill in Southborough.

One Esquire in particular should also be singled out, partly because of his relevance to Tunbridge Wells and partly because his patronage marked a change in the direction of Burton's professional career. John Ward, JP, DL, MP (1776-1855) of Devonshire Place, St.Marylebone, and Holwood, Kent, also had a property interest in Regent's Park (5) as well as in Tunbridge Wells. Holwood at Keston, was designed by Burton for Ward in 1823-6 in a Palladian form, with widely spaced wings connected to a central block and some confident Grecian detailing. (See page 50).

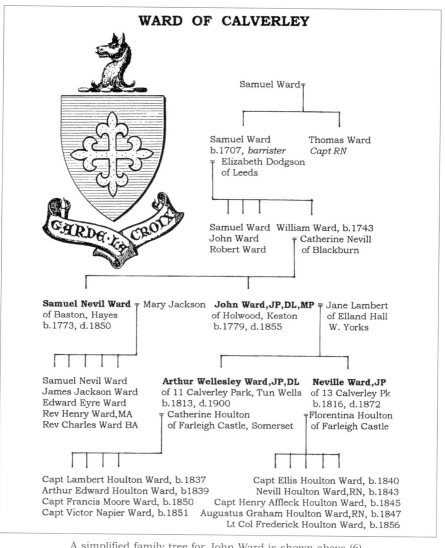

WARD OF CALVERLEY

Samuel Ward

Samuel Ward
b.1707, *barrister*
⊤ Elizabeth Dodgson
of Leeds

Thomas Ward
Capt RN

Samuel Ward
John Ward
Robert Ward

William Ward, b.1743
⊤ Catherine Nevill
of Blackburn

Samuel Nevil Ward ⊤ Mary Jackson
of Baston, Hayes
b.1773, d.1850

John Ward, JP, DL, MP ⊤ Jane Lambert
of Holwood, Keston   of Elland Hall
b.1779, d.1855   W. Yorks

Samuel Nevil Ward
James Jackson Ward
Edward Eyre Ward
Rev Henry Ward, MA
Rev Charles Ward BA

Arthur Wellesley Ward, JP, DL
of 11 Calverley Park, Tun Wells
b.1813, d.1900
⊤ Catherine Houlton
of Farleigh Castle, Somerset

Neville Ward, JP
of 13 Calverley Pk
b.1816, d.1872
⊤ Florentina Houlton
of Farleigh Castle

Capt Lambert Houlton Ward, b.1837
Arthur Edward Houlton Ward, b1839
Capt Francis Moore Ward, b.1850
Capt Victor Napier Ward, b.1851

Capt Ellis Houlton Ward, b.1840
Nevill Houlton Ward, RN, b.1843
Capt Henry Affleck Houlton Ward, b.1845
Augustus Graham Houlton Ward, RN, b.1847
Lt Col Frederick Houlton Ward, b.1856

A simplified family tree for John Ward is shown above (6).

Burton also did work for John Ward's elder brother, Samuel Nevil Ward, at Baston House, Hayes, near Holwood at Keston. Burton subsequently adopted the name "Baston" for his own property in Tunbridge Wells. John Ward was a Justice of the Peace and Deputy Lieutenant for the County of Kent, serving as High Sheriff in 1835, and was MP for Leominster in 1830 (7).

A handwritten list of Burton's works, preserved in Hastings Museum, lists "Tunbridge Wells Calverley Estate – J. Ward" but, also, "T.Wells Calverley Park Villas designs – Messrs. Bramah". Similarly, Burton's obituary in "The Builder" lists, under 1828-52, "Tunbridge Wells, Calverley improvements – Mr John Ward" and under 1828-30 "Tunbridge Wells, Calverley Park, villas, etc. designs – Messrs. Bramah" (8). Thus it appears that, while Ward was the client for the overall Calverley development, the clients for at least some of the individual villas in Calverley Park was more likely to have been Messrs. Bramah.

By an agreement between John Ward and Messrs. Bramah, dated 3rd April 1829, leases were assigned to Timothy, Francis, Edward and John Joseph Bramah on land in Calverley Park for 72 years from 29th September 1828, at a peppercorn rent for the first eight years (9).

The four Bramah brothers, of Pimlico in London, were in a business co-partnership and described themselves as "Engineers, Blacksmiths, and Plumbers" (10). The business, it seems, prospered and enabled them to go into property development in this way. Bramahs set up Tunbridge Wells workshops in Camden Road, in the vicinity of the present Prince of Wales Public House, and stone for building on the Calverley Estate came from the quarry on the estate, in the vicinity of what is now Quarry Road. Bramahs held an office at 6 Calverley Place (11), a building that still exists but renumbered as 67 Calverley Road.

The firm of Bramah and Co. survived well into the 20th century, although as lock-smiths (12), rather than as building contractors or property developers. Most obvious today of their metalwork achieve-ments are the magnificent iron gates designed by Burton for the Wellington Arch at London's Hyde Park Corner. (To the right, part of the decorative ironwork).

CHAPTER 3

REGENCY NEO-CLASSICISM

Decimus Burton's first major public building was the Colosseum in Regent's Park (1823-7, demolished 1875) with a dome rather larger than that of St.Paul's Cathedral. A Grecian version of the Pantheon in Rome, the building met with considerable praise at the time. James Elmes, in "Metropolitan Improvements" described its portico as "one of the finest and best proportioned of Greco-Doric in the Metropolis" (1) and soon afterwards important commissions in the Royal Parks followed from the Office of Woods and Forests.

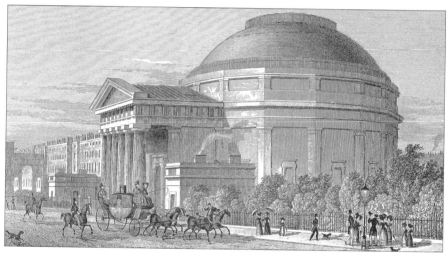

Colosseum, Regent's Park built 1823-1827, demolished 1875

In 1825 Burton was commissioned, through that Office, to provide designs for works in London's Hyde Park, including the Ionic Screen at

Hyde Park Corner. This triple screen has a central arched feature, linked to side arches by colonnades. Above the central arch is a series of classical reliefs by John Henning the Younger.

The Ionic Screen, or 'Façade' at Hyde Park Corner, 1826

Originally aligned on the same axis as the screen was a Roman style Triumphal Arch, now known as the Wellington Arch, which was intended as an entrance to Buckingham Palace from the north.

Drawn by Thos H. Shepherd.

Engraved by J. Cleghorn.

The Wellington Arch, Hyde Park Corner, 1826

The Arch has a single opening, with Corinthian columns on either side, a similar form to the first century Arch of Titus in Rome. The crowning quadriga of Burton's arch was replaced for a while, much to his distress, by an out-of-scale sideways-on, gigantic statue of the Duke of Wellington. In 1883, however, the whole arch structure was moved to its present position, and the statue removed to Aldershot. The magnificent iron gates, designed by Burton and made by Messrs. Bramah, bear the name Bramah and Sons beneath the Royal Arms.

The Wellington Arch, when surmounted by a 28 ft. high statue of the Duke of Wellington. Burton disliked this intensely and at one stage left a £2,000 bequest in his will (about £100-£150,000 at today's values) towards its removal.

Undoubtedly one of the most interesting of Burton's buildings is the Athenaeum Club of 1827-30, at the corner of London's Pall Mall and Waterloo Place. Here, Burton can be seen combining Grecian and Roman elements to remarkable effect. Externally, the form of the building adopted has something of the character of a Palazzo of the Italian Renaissance, and Sir John Summerson has suggested that it may have a hint of Peruzzi's 17th century Palazzo Pietro Massimi in Rome (2). Above a continuous balcony dividing the two original storeys, the first floor is astylar, with a Parthenaic frieze by John Henning the Elder. Internally, the various main rooms of the Club are grouped symmetrically around a central staircase, rather as they might be in a country house. The entrance hall again combines Roman and Grecian tastes, with Greek Corinthian columns, modelled on the Tower of the Winds in Athens, supporting a richly coffered Roman-style barrel-vaulted ceiling.

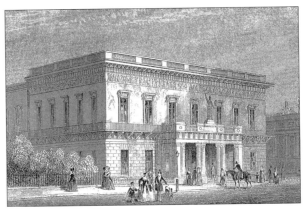

The Athenaeum Club, Waterloo Place, 1827-30

Another of Burton's major public buildings is the former Charing Cross Hospital, now a police station, adjacent to John Nash's West Strand improvements. It is with such prominent classical works that the Regency period is frequently associated, and Burton, along with such names as Soane, Smirke, Wilkins, Nash and Basevi, ranks as one of its principal practitioners.

The former Charing Cross Hospital

CHAPTER 4

CALVERLEY NEW TOWN

Decimus Burton's obituary in "The Builder" magazine opines that "Mr Burton's public works would probably have been more numerous and important had he not been early tempted by the offer of Mr John Ward, of Tunbridge Wells, from whom he accepted a special retainer to lay out for him the Calverley Park Estate. This engagement occupied most of his time for some years………" (1).

The death had occurred on 31st December 1823 of Thomas Panuwell, "late of Mount Calverley" (2). Panuwell had owned a considerable area of land, and his estate extended from "Calverley's Plain", Tunbridge Wells, (3) north-eastwards to Pembury. This land was bought by John Ward in 1826 for the sum of £24,135 (4). Ward had already bought three other contiguous parcels of land, namely the Jack Wood's spring and quarry, – also in 1826; the Lanthorn House lands, where the Town Hall now stands, in 1825; and, also in 1825, the Great Mount Pleasant Estate including Calverley House, later to be occupied by Princess Victoria and her mother, the Duchess of Kent. Thus, by the end of 1826 Ward had put together the 874 acre Calverley Estate, so elegantly recorded in the Estate Plan prepared by the Surveyor W. Craggs in 1829 and preserved in Tunbridge Wells Museum.

Of this extensive estate, 56 acres at its eastern end were earmarked for building. The aim was "to erect a number of edifices suitable to the reception of genteel families; and simultaneously with the larger buildings, a number of shops, etc. in their immediate neighbourhood, so that the residents upon this estate might enjoy the same advantages as those who lived nearer the Springs" (5). Burton laid out the development in 1828 and a plan of 1832 is illustrated on page 24 (6). This shows the shops and houses numbered 65-79 Calverley Road (Calverley Place) in being by that time; together with Nos. 1-11 of the Calverley Park villas; Calverley Terrace, facing Crescent Road; and Calverley Parade, facing Mount Pleasant Road. Bramah's Workshops existed in Camden Road, but the site of Calverley Park Crescent was shown as "Proposed Calverley Promenade".

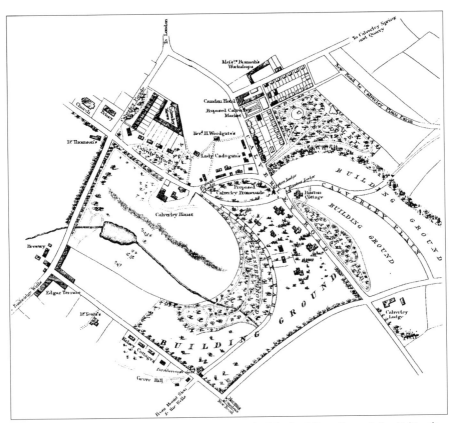

Plan of that part of the Calverley Estate earmarked for building. From John Britton's
'Descriptive Sketches of Tunbridge Wells and the Calverley Estate', 1832

The Calverley Park villas, in their landscaped setting were arranged
in an arc, facing a pleasure ground. Thus the occupants could enjoy
the illusion of looking out from their front windows over ancestral
acres. The veteran topographer and friend of Sir John Soane, John
Britton FSA, says of the Calverley Park villas in his "Descriptive
sketches of Tunbridge Wells and the Calverley Estate", "in designing
and placing these houses the architect has evidently studied variety,
but restrained his fancy to such simple forms and sizes as seemed
best adapted to an economical expenditure" (7). The variety within the
range of "simple forms" is illustrated in the sketches shown on pages
26 and 27.

24

Italianate, Grecian, Old English and Gothic co-exist harmoniously side by side, and the experience of walking along the curved carriage drive can be likened to turning the pages of a late Georgian architectural pattern book.

Broadly speaking, the single and paired villas numbered 5 and 6, 7, 9 and 10, 13, 14, 15, 20 and 21 Calverley Park could be described as being in the traditions of classical proportion derived from the long, uninterrupted reign of Georgian architecture. Thus these may appear as archetypal Regency villas, especially where curved canopies and architectural ironwork of the period strengthen that image.

Burton indulged in a number of asymmetrical compositions too, as may be seen at nos. 2, 11, 16, 18, 19 and 22. Italianate in feeling stylistically are nos. 1, 8, 17 and 23, with their triple windows and bracketed eaves. The pointed arches of nos. 12 and 24 introduce 'Gothick' touches, while nos. 3 and 4, with their high-pitched roofs, decorative bargeboards and Tudoresque details, come into the "Old English" category.

John Ward's two sons, Arthur Wellesley Ward and Neville Ward, were living at nos. 11 and 13 Calverley Park in the 1840s (8). Both, like Decimus Burton, who took possession of no. 4 Calverley Park in 1835 (9), were Commissioners under the Tunbridge Wells Improvement Act. By the time the Tithe Map and Colbran's 1839 map of Tunbridge Wells were produced, all twenty-four of the Calverley Park villas were complete.

As Prof. Henry Russell Hitchcock has observed, it was "definitely a late Georgian, not a Victorian realisation" (10) of the idea of a loose grouping of residential villas arranged around an open park. Probably, concludes Prof. Hitchcock, "the finest extant example" (11) of its kind.

No.1, Calverley Park, from Britton's
'Topographical Sketches of Tunbridge Wells'

Although nos. 3, 15, 16, 17, 23 and 24 Calverley Park were requisitioned during the Second World War, the whole of Calverley Park remained in the hands of the Ward family until after the cessation of hostilities.

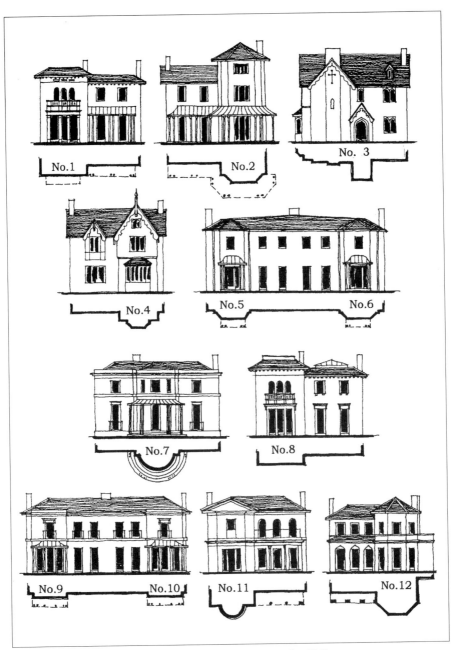

Nos. 1-24 Calverley Park, Tunbridge Wells.
Illustration of the variety in composition, façade and profile

26

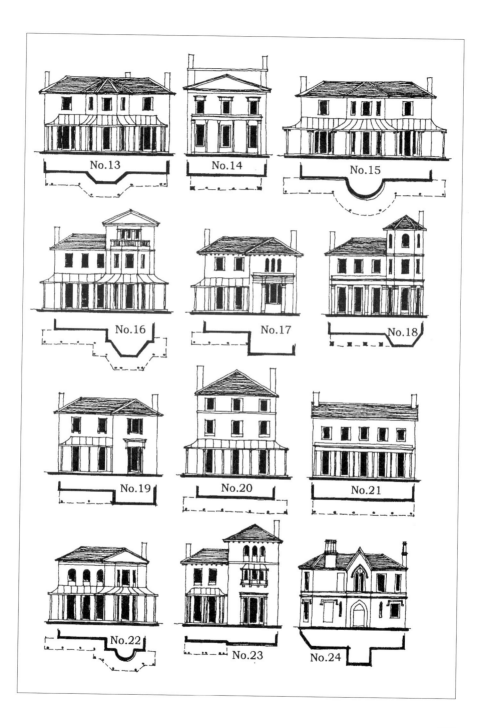

No.13 No.14 No.15 No.16 No.17 No.18 No.19 No.20 No.21 No.22 No.23 No.24

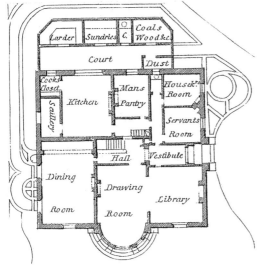

Auction sale particulars of 30th November 1945 state that the policy of the Ward Estate had been "to modernise each residence as opportunity arose without destroying its attractive Georgian features" (12). Modernisation could include such matters as bringing kitchens up from basement to ground floor level, and the present relatively unspoiled appearance of the Park owes much to the policy applied by the estate owners for more than a century.

No.7 Calverley Park: View and Plan

Two of the three lodges to the Park are classical in style. Burton is relatively sparing in his use of the Orders of Architecture in Calverley Park, but Victoria Lodge has Greek Doric pavilions on either side of the Roman entrance arch.

Victoria Gate and Lodge, Calverley Park, Tunbridge Wells

Keston Lodge, like the Tower of the Winds in Athens is octagonal in plan, but has round arched and circular openings.

Keston Lodge to Calverley Park, Tunbridge Wells

Farnborough Lodge, at the Grove Hill Road end of the Park is rustic in style, of which more in Chapter 5.

While Calverley Park remains virtually intact, all that survives of Calverley Parade and Calverley Terrace are the wall in front of the Civic Centre complex and the pair of houses now numbered 9 and 10 Crescent Road.

Calverley Parade, Tunbridge Wells

Calverley Terrace, Tunbridge Wells

Burton's Market House (later the Old Town Hall and then the School of Arts and Crafts), the former Camden Hotel, and Bramah's workshops in Camden Road also do not survive.

The sequence of shops and houses now nos. 57-79 Calverley Road, but formerly known as Calverley Place, does however survive, and originally took the form of three-storied pavilions, linked by single-storied shops.

Calverley Place, now 57-79 Calverley Road   Detail of one of the linked pavilions

Behind Calverley Place are Calverley Cottages, now numbered 6-20 Garden Street. Occupants of these in the 1840s included a gamekeeper, a laundress, a gardener, a bricklayer, a painter and a sawyer (13). The cottages have tooled ashlar on their Garden Street frontages and coursed rubble with ashlar dressings on the flank elevations. Nos. 10 and 12 have been rebuilt.

Calverley Cottages:
Elevations and Plan

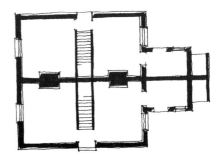

Calverley Park Crescent was first called Calverley Promenade and originally contained shops on the ground floor, with lodgings on the upper floors.

Calverley Park Crescent
from a mid-Victorian illustration by Rock & Co

Britton's map of 1832 shows the property as "proposed", but it must have been erected soon afterwards, for the following description appeared under the title 'Calverley Promenade' in "The Tunbridge Wells Visitor" in April 1834 (14):

"An elegant range of seventeen Shops, with convenient Private Residences over the Shops, has been erected at the North-west portion of Calverley Park, on the plan of a Crescent, having a spacious Colonnade in front, opening at each end to the public road. The Colonnade is supported by light iron pillars, so as to combine the convenience of shelter with a handsome appearance. The aspect is South-east, looking over the Park, beautiful distant scenery, rendering the houses highly eligible for Lodgings.

It will be seen, on inspecting the Buildings, that the Colonnade towards the Park being raised one story high above the level of Hervey Road, gives the opportunity to each householder of having another Shop on the lower floor towards Hervey Road, which would be applicable for those trades which could not be admitted on the Colonnade.

A large extent of Pleasure-Ground, attached to and in front of the Building, is laid out; where it is proposed that the company should also be allowed to promenade, and in which, during the season, a Band of Musicians may be placed.

It is intended that the support and management of the Pleasure-Ground, &c. be vested in a Committee to be chosen amongst the Householders, who naturally would be most interested in the success, and by preventing annoyances, endeavour to render it the resort of the respectable and fashionable.

Parties desirous of taking Houses or Shops, may obtain further particulars, and view the Plans, at Messrs. Bramah's Counting-houses, London and Tunbridge Wells."

Already, by then, some of the premises were occupied. The central feature originally designed with a crowning pediment, was the Calverley Library and Reading Room at No.9, where newspapers and reviews could be perused or books borrowed. Also, books could be

bought and pianos and globes hired (15). At No.1 Calverley Park Crescent, the Royal Baths offered shampooing, medicated vapour, aromatic, sulphur, borage, nitro-muriatic acid, tepid, douche, and shower baths (16). Other traders included a tailor at No.13 and fancy goods at No.2 (17). Messrs. Bramah were clearly involved in the development, as particulars of available properties in the Crescent could be obtained from their office at 6 Calverley Place (18). The process of converting the shops into residential accommodation seems to have started in about 1837 (19).

In 1834 "The Tunbridge Wells Visitor" carried an advertisement addressed to "Hotel Keepers, Builders, Wine Merchants, and others" offering Calverley House, Mount Pleasant, for conversion into a hotel

(20). The advertisement added that the Proprietor was ready to advance half of the estimated cost of necessary additional buildings, and that further particulars could be had at Decimus Burton's office. Colbran's New Guide for 1839 describes the Hotel as "recently finished" (21). The Hotel was originally named The Calverley, but more recently the Hôtel du Vin.

Calverley House, then the Calverley Hotel, later the Hôtel du Vin.

The same guide comments on Decimus Burton's designs for the Calverley Estate that "as the buildings progressed, it was evident that a new town was springing up" (22). To the shops, houses and other buildings of the new town was added in 1834 the Victoria National School. The ceremony of laying the first stone of this Tudor Gothic style building was performed on 29th September 1834 by no lesser persons than the young Princess Victoria and her mother, the Duchess of Kent (23). At this, the plans of the building were explained to their Royal Highnesses and the Duchess expressed her satisfaction regarding Decimus Burton's design. Their Royal Highnesses donated the sum of £100 towards the cost of the building and, at a General Meeting of Subscribers held at the School Room on 4th April 1835, the thanks of the meeting were voted to Decimus Burton for the gratuity of his professional services in connection with this charitable object. (24)

Victoria National School

Quatrefoil border based on former loggia at Burrswood

CHAPTER 5

RUSTIC AND PICTURESQUE

Reference was made in the last chapter to the rustic Farnborough Lodge in Tunbridge Wells' Calverley Park, and it is as a master not only of the neo-classical but also of the picturesque that Decimus Burton should be remembered.

Burton was no stranger to the art of the landscape designer and he co-operated closely with the leading landscape designers of his time. These included William Nesfield at Kew Gardens and Robert Marnock (1800-1889) in London's Regent's Park (1). Marnock's name is well known in Tunbridge Wells for his work at Dunorlan Park. In Calverley Park the pleasure grounds were laid out in a picturesque manner, with meandering paths, and were complemented with the picturesque Farnborough Lodge (right). This little structure has lost its rustic work loggia, decorative bargeboards and finial, but otherwise it remains intact.

Sadly, the pleasure grounds in Calverley Plain (now Calverley Park Gardens), described in Colbran's Guide of 1840 as "laid out with great taste" (2) are no more.

Baston Cottage – Entrance elevation to Calverley Plain (Calverley Park Gardens) – based on an original drawing in Hastings Museum

Neither, even more sadly, is its associated Baston Cottage, described by Colbran as "an elegant building in the Gothic style of architecture........the property of Decimus Burton Esq." (3).

Soane's friend John Britton also comments upon the "beautiful pleasure-garden" in Calverley Plain, "adorned with various evergreens, flowers, etc." (4), adding that "at one extremity of this ground Mr. Decimus Burton has built a rustic cottage for himself" (5). Britton illustrates two views of the building and two more are preserved in Hastings Museum.

Garden elevation of Decimus Burton's Baston Cottage in Calverley Plain, from a painting in Hastings Museum.

Between them they give an interesting insight into the mind of an architect, sometimes stereotyped as feeling no enthusiasm for the Gothic Revival, when satisfying his own caprices as his own client. Highly picturesque, the building had decorative chimneys, finials and bargeboards, pointed windows, rustic-work loggias and roofs which were partly tiled and partly thatched, perhaps deliberately giving the effect of a building that had grown organically.

South elevation of 'The Grove', Penshurst, based upon the original contract drawings of 1828

While Baston Cottage has been lost to the Tunbridge Wells scene for the past century, three other Burton buildings in that genre do survive in the vicinity, although all have complications in their building histories.

The very pretty "cottage orné named "The Grove" at Penshurst is a particularly well documented example, dating from 1828-33. The original contract drawings, specification and much correspondence are preserved in the Centre for Kentish Studies at Maidstone.

Also in the "Old English" manner is Burrswood, at Groombridge, which dates from the 1830s. In his County History of 1838,

Burrswood circa 1840

C. Greenwood describes Burrswood, the seat of David Salomons, as "a handsome structure, chiefly in the Elizabethan style, recently erected under the professional superintendence of Decimus Burton, Esq." A view of Burrswood at about that time is preserved in the Memento Room at David Salomons' House at Broomhill, Southborough. This shows a rural residence with a picturesque garden front, having a central gothick loggia, canopies and a set-back gothick conservatory (7). The now familiar sequence of gabled roofs, tall chimneys and mullioned windows may have taken shape towards the end of

Burrswood – the sequence of gables now familiar today.

Salomons' ownership of Burrswood around the mid-19th century; and these developments could be seen as part of the architectural movement that produced high-Victorian works such as George Devey's St. Alban's Court, Nonnington, Kent, a decade or more later.

Deveyesque too, is Bentham Hill, Southborough, of 1832-3. Although Burton's original design has been complicated by 20th century alterations, Burton's hand is strongly in evidence and the hipped and gabled roofs, together with the chimneys, give not only a picturesque effect, but the impression of a building that has developed organically over time. In 1838, Greenwood described the building as " an elegant modern structure, partly Elizabethan, with a mixture of cottage style, from a design of Decimus Burton, Esq."(8) One divided chimney stack served a fireplace with a window above, a feature perpetuated in the 20th century changes. Burton used this intriguing arrangement in the design of his own Baston Cottage and, to great effect, at Burrswood.

The east elevation at Bentham Hill has the date 1833 in its central gable, and the north elevation rests on a heavily rusticated basement with four-centred arched openings. Most unusual for its date is the large canted porch, set in angle of the building's south-west frontage. A sketch plan among the Burton papers in Hastings Museum shows such a porch and appears to be an early idea for this extraordinarily interesting house that is Bentham Hill. The property remained in the hands of the original Pott family until the early part of the 20th. century and is now in seven flats.

Bentham Hill, Southborough, 1832-33, before the 20th. century alterations

Another picturesque house by Burton, Spring Grove at Pembury of 1829-30, was unfortunately demolished in the later 19th century. It was, again, "Old English" in character with a large gable and decorative bargeboards on the park front (9).

Other more formal domestic works in the area were Mitchells, now Holmewood, at Langton Green (1827), much rebuilt; Great Culverden, Tunbridge Wells (1827), now demolished; Broomhill at Southborough (1831-8), greatly extended; and Hollands, at Langton Green (1835-6).

While Burton was engaged upon the development of the Calverley Estate and the domestic architecture in and around Tunbridge Wells, he was also working to great picturesque effect on London Zoo. On 5th May 1826, the year of its formation, the Zoological Society of London appointed a Committee consisting of Lord Auckland, Sir Humphrey Davy and Sir Stamford Raffles to undertake the management of the planned grounds and buildings in Regents Park and, on 3rd June, a sketch layout was passed, the President being asked to be in touch with Burton and to take matters forward (10). Burton's formal appointment as Architect to the Society came in 1830 (11), a post which he continued to occupy for the next eleven years.

The original site, five acres in extent on the south side of the Outer Circle was laid out by Burton in a picturesque manner with meandering paths, and was opened in April 1828 (12). Burton's early animal houses were of a "cottage orné" character designed

Thatched elephant stables, 1830-31

to fit in with the picturesque nature of the gardens. Among these, the Elephant House of 1830-31 had a thatched roof and "gothick" openings. The Llama House too was in the gothick style and incorporated a rustic-work loggia on one side.

In indicating his willingness to accept the office of Architect to the Society, Burton expressed concern to have control over the Gardener

Gothic house for Llamas

and the Carpenter who, clearly, must have been the key figures in the execution of his landscape and building designs. The combination of timber construction and changing attitudes to animal husbandry has meant that knowledge about these early buildings is only available from illustrations, including a splendid series of views drawn in 1834 by James Hakewill.

By 1836-37 Burton was building the more substantial and functional Giraffe House, in stock brick, with its tall round-headed stable doors, and this does survive, despite war damage and alterations. The Clock Tower too, owes its basic form to Burton's Llama and subsequently Camel House, although reconstructed following bomb damage. Other survivals from the Burton era include the Macaw Aviary, or Raven cage, and the East tunnel entrance.

Also, while busy with his projects in and around Tunbridge Wells, Burton laid out Beulah Spa in Norwood, near Croydon, in a picturesque manner. An account of the Saline Spa of 1832 reads:

"the grounds are entered at a rustic lodge" and have been "laid out under the direction, and adorned by the chaste and elegant taste of Mr. Decimus Burton. Rustic edifices, in graceful keeping with the natural beauties of the spot, embellish its finest points of view, and walks and drives traverse the sylvan scene, varying with picturesque effect the wildness of the landscape" (13).

An intriguing scheme for a rustic village of detached gothic villas set in their own grounds at Furze Hill, Brighton, can only be seen from an engraving by J.S. Templeton of circa 1830 (14).

CHAPTER 6

HOUSES OF PRAYER

In 1827, Decimus Burton exhibited at the Royal Academy both his famous classical works at London's Hyde Park Corner, and also his gothic Trinity Church in Tunbridge Wells, "now being erected" (1). Then, in 1829, the new church featured in the Academy again, this time with Calverley Park and other of Burton's Tunbridge Wells buildings. It does need to be kept firmly in mind that Trinity is a Georgian building and not a Victorian one.

Trinity Church, Tunbridge Wells, 1827-29

During Victoria's reign, large numbers of Gothic Revival churches were built by architects such as Sir George Gilbert Scott and G.E. Street. Before the 1820s, however, new Gothic Revival churches were relatively unusual. It was only in 1817 that the architect Thomas

Rickman (1776-1841) produced his publication "An attempt to Discriminate the Styles of English Architecture from the Conquest to the Reformation", coining the terms "Early English", "Decorated" and "Perpendicular" that have remained accepted nomenclature ever since.

The Pointed Styles adopted for Trinity were the "Early English" and "Decorated" of the 13th and 14th centuries, rather than the "Perpendicular" of the 15th century, when some saw the Gothic style as being in decline.

The architectural historian Professor Mark Girouard has suggested that there are two types of Gothic in the 19th century: imitative and creative Gothic. Trinity, Girouard puts firmly in the creative category and perhaps there is much in the interesting suggestion made by the architectural writer Marcus Binney of "Country Life" that at a time when most building in Gothic tended towards the filigree and the light-weight, Burton sought to imbue Trinity with an almost primitive forcefulness by exaggerating and simplifying the traditional elements of the Gothic Vocabulary. Certainly, the traditional elements of the Gothic Vocabulary are present and a walk around Trinity can at times seem fascinatingly like turning the pages of A.C.Pugin's

Plan of Trinity Church, Tunbridge Wells

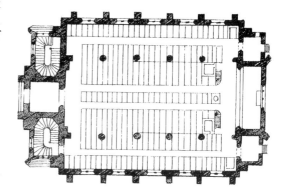

Trinity Church and The Priory Houses, Tunbridge Wells from Britton's "Descriptive Sketches of Tunbridge Wells", 1832

"Specimens of Gothic Architecture" as dripstone terminals, tracery, moulded "capitals", and other features meet one's gaze (2).

East window of Trinity Church, Tunbridge Wells, 1827   Example from A. C. Pugin's "Specimens of Gothic Architecture", 1823

A.C. Pugin, father of the architect A.W.N. Pugin, was a draughtsman in Nash's office, so it would not be surprising for Burton to be familiar with his work. The mouldings of alternate capitals at Trinity are not unlike a 13th century Early English example from Southwark Cathedral, illustrated by A.C. Pugin in his "Specimens". The East window, too, is not dissimilar to a 14th century example with curvilinear tracery, from St.Mary Magdalen Church, Oxford, and it is advanced for its date of 1827.

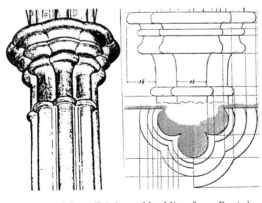

Nave capital from Trinity Church, Tunbridge Wells, 1827   Moulding from Pugin's "Specimens", 1823

Trinity was admired at the time of its building and was described in the periodical "John Bull" as a "beautiful structure" (3), while Clifford's Visitor's Guide for Tunbridge Wells states: "Trinity Church, situated nearly in the centre of the place, is a handsome structure, and reflects great credit on the architect, Mr. Decimus Burton" (4). Colbran, too, calls the structure "handsome" (5).

By 1937 Margaret Barton wrote, in her book on Tunbridge Wells: "Tastes change bewilderingly, and many neo-Gothic churches of this period, held in the utmost contempt in the lifetimes of most of us, have come back into favour. But it is inconceivable that this clumsy box-like building,......... could be admired in any age." (6).

Trinity Church from the North West

Interior before conversion into an Arts Centre

Bewildering at the start of the new Millennium is the way in which a building which was well received at the time and which is currently admired, and "listed" by the government in the top category, could have been so vilified during the intervening period. The "box-like" form of which Margaret Barton complains is characteristic of "Commissioners' Churches" of which Trinity is a good example (7). Some two thirds of the £12,000 cost of building Trinity came from a Parliamentary grant, through the Church Building Commission.

Seating was provided in the church for 1,500 persons and part of the challenge to architects in such cases was to accommodate a large number of people in a rectangular space, while providing an acceptable architectural display and keeping within spending limits. On all three counts Burton could be said to have acquitted himself well.

43

Declared pastorally redundant by the Church authorities in 1972, Trinity re-opened as an Arts Centre in 1982. Immediately to the east of the building are the very pretty "Gothick" Priory Houses which, although now truncated at their eastern end, form an attractive group with the church.

Although Decimus Burton did produce some classical church designs, his executed ecclesiastical works are gothic in style and mainly of a simple "Early English" lancet type.

St. Peter's Church, South-borough, Kent, of 1830 was, in its original form, a characteristic example of the genre and, in his essay on the Gothic Revival, Sir Kenneth Clark refers to Southborough Church, along with St. Michael's, Bath (8). As with some other of Burton's churches, however, the simplicity of his original work has been complicated by later alterations.

St. Peter's Church, Southborough, before the 1880s alterations

St Mary's Church, Riverhead, Kent, of 1831 remains, despite later changes at its eastern end, very much a Burton building (9) and is, arguably, one of his best churches after Trinity Church in Tunbridge

St. Mary's, Riverhead

Wells. Standing on high ground, approached by a steep flight of steps, the west front is an impressive sight as the building is approached from Worships Hill opposite. The west door, at the top of the flight of steps, has stiff-leaf capitals on either side and is set in a western tower which is surmounted by a spire and four of Burton's obelisk pinnacles. More corner pinnacles mark the ends of the sloping roofs on either side. The interior is good too, with a plaster rib-vaulted nave. Again, it needs to be kept in mind that St.Mary's is not a Victorian building. It dates from the year that George IV died and William IV started his seven year reign.

44

Somewhat later are the three Sussex churches:

- ❖ *St.Mary's, Goring-by-Sea,* 1836-8 but incorporating some earlier work;

- ❖ *Holy Trinity, Eastbourne,* built in 1837-9 as Trinity District Chapel (10), but later greatly extended;

- ❖ and *St. Augustine's, Flimwell* of 1839, with its open hammerbeam roof (11).

St.Augustine's, too, has been extended, the chancel and the spire being subsequent work. Internally, the hammer-posts of Burton's nave have ornamental drop-pendants, and the collar braces which rise from the ends of the hammer-beams form a four-centred arch, supporting a king-post. Externally, substantial buttresses divide the nave into three bays, each bay containing paired lancets, and a corbel-table supporting the eaves.

Immediately to the west of St.Augustine's, the Old Vicarage is contemporary with the church (12) and also has been attributed to Burton. The stone building is very much in Burton's Old English style, with decorative bargeboards to the gable on the north front, stone copings to the two gables on the east elevation, late Tudor-style window and chimney details, and fish-scale tiling to the roof.

St.Peter's Church, Fleetwood, Lancashire, 1840; and *St.Mary's, Bradford Peverell,* 1849-51 are, again, both gothick in style.

While the new Trinity Church in Tunbridge Wells was nearing completion, Decimus Burton was also called upon to act in connection with repairs to the Chapel of King Charles the Martyr in the town. In April 1829 the Minister, Revd. W. Pope, laid before a meeting of the Chapel Trustees a report by Burton reflecting the state of repair of the structure (13). Burton himself attended a meeting of the Trustees on 30th May 1829 and he was paid the sum of £18.19s.0d. for his report, drawings and superintendence of the works.

Burton also was involved, jointly with Sidney Smirke, in the restoration of the Temple Church in London in 1841-3. Following differences between the previous architect, James Savage, and the Building Committee of Benchers, responsibility for repairs and restoration was transferred to Decimus Burton on behalf of the Middle Temple and Sidney Smirke on behalf of the Inner Temple. (14).

The Old Vicarage, to the west of
St. Augustine's Church, Flimwell

CHAPTER 7

TOWN PLANNING AND UTOPIA

"A New Lanark by the Sea" was the title of an article on the town of Fleetwood, Lancashire, which appeared in "Country Life" in 1975 (1).

Now a World Heritage Site, New Lanark, in Scotland, owes its international fame to the Utopian ideas of the visionary Robert Owen (1771-1858). Owen sought to change the nature of the post-Napoleonic War industrial structure, and to devote as much attention to the human machine as to the machinery on the factory floor. At New Lanark, Owen had inherited a straggling village but, in setting out his theories, he envisaged new "villages of cooperation" planned on geometrical lines.

So when, in the mid-1830s he and Sir Peter Hesketh-Fleetwood were exploring the idea of a second New Lanark on Sir Peter's Rossall Estate in Lancashire, it was perhaps not too surprising that a geometrical plan should emerge. The idea behind the new town of Fleetwood was that it should not only be a sea-side watering place and a commercial port but, importantly, a key part of a route from London to Scotland, by rail to Fleetwood via Preston, and thence by sea to Glasgow. Burton produced a remarkable geometrical plan, with radial roads embodying some of the Utopian ideas put forward by Renaissance architects in 16th century Italy.

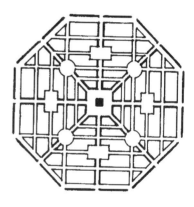

A Renaissance 'ideal plan'
(Giorgio Vasari 1511-74)

Alas for Fleetwood, railway engineering conquered the Cumbrian Fells as early as 1847, providing a direct rail link to Scotland. Thus, although part of Burton's street layout exists, the Fleetwood of today tends to be rather a case of what might have been. Surviving Burton buildings include the classical North Euston Hotel and the very delightful Little Pharos Lighthouse.

47

North Euston Hotel, Fleetwood, 1841   Little Pharos Lighthouse

Fleetwood on Wyre

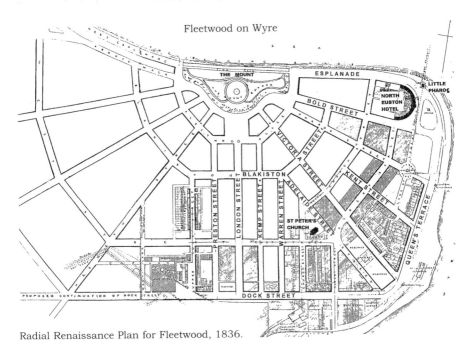

Radial Renaissance Plan for Fleetwood, 1836.

In addition to his major town planning schemes at Tunbridge Wells and at Fleetwood, Burton was involved in a number of other planning and estate schemes, some of which bore fruit under his supervision, while others were precursors to later developments. Most notable among those displaying surviving Burton buildings is Queen Adelaide Crescent of 1830-34 in Brighton. Here, in 1830-34, Decimus Burton, the neo-classical Regency architect, seemed to be anticipating what Osbert Lancaster came to categorize as "Kensington Italianate". Burton exhibited his design for Queen Adelaide Crescent at the Royal Academy in 1831 and visited the site at least twice in 1833, while building work on nos. 1-10 was in progress (2).

Also in the 1830s Burton was commissioned by the 2nd Earl of Burlington, afterwards the 7th Duke of Devonshire, to prepare a plan for the development of his Compton Estate at Eastbourne (3). However, it was not until the coming of the railway that Eastbourne burgeoned, and it fell to Burton's pupil Henry Currey (1820-1900) to take matters forward there.

In 1840 Matthew Montgomerie acquired the Kelvinside Estate in Glasgow and Decimus Burton was appointed as the Estate Architect (4). Burton's plan for the area envisaged terraces lining Great Western Road, close to the Botanic Garden, with villas in a landscape setting behind.

At Folkestone, Burton prepared an Estate Plan for the 3rd Earl of Radnor (5), covering The Leas area, in 1843. From 1845 until 1859 he acted as Architect to the Gervis Estate in Bournemouth (6), where extensive pleasure gardens line Gervis Place and Westover Road.

Rosette border, based on ironwork at the Palm House, Kew

CHAPTER 8

GLASS HOUSES AND CONSERVATORIES

From the earliest days of Decimus Burton's professional career, conservatories or green-houses had featured in his work.

In 1816, when J.C. Loudon was experimenting with iron sash bars to make English hot-houses look beautiful in their own right, instead of being merely lean-to glazed sheds (1), the youthful Burton was involved with his first work, namely The Holme in London's Regent's Park. The conservatory there could be seen as coming into the glazed lean-to category but in 1823 the "greenhouse" at Holwood, Keston, for John Ward, was fully integrated into the architectural composition, complete with Doric columns and a pediment.

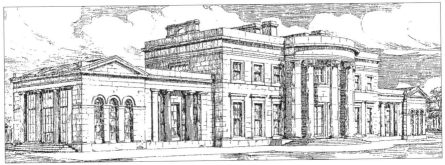

Holwood, Keston 1823

At Blackhurst in Tunbridge Wells the original conservatory was more than a mere shed and it seems that Burrswood, Groombridge, once had a Gothic conservatory. The full flowering of Burton's domestic

Blackhurst

conservatory came at Grimston, Yorkshire, where cast-iron columns in the form of palm trees supported an elegant glazed domed roof (2).

The survival rate of conservatories tends not to be high and, of the great glass houses, Burton's Winter Garden in London's Regent's Park and the Paxton/Burton Great Conservatory at Chatsworth no longer remain. However, Burton's work at the Royal Botanic Gardens, Kew, is still there to be enjoyed and must rank alongside his neo-classical monuments and his domestic schemes as one of his three principal claims to fame.

On 5th July 1844 Decimus Burton wrote to Sir William Hooker, the first Director of Kew Gardens, informing him that the Treasury had authorized acceptance of Richard Turner's tender for the Palm House, "provided he can provide satisfactory securities for the performance"

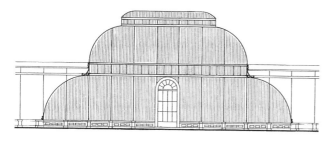

(3). Completed in 1848 the building has been described as "one of the boldest pieces of 19th century functionalism in existence – much bolder indeed, and hence aesthetically much more satisfying than the Crystal Palace ever was "(4).

Arguably, the Palm House could have a just claim as the world's most important surviving Victorian glass and iron structure.

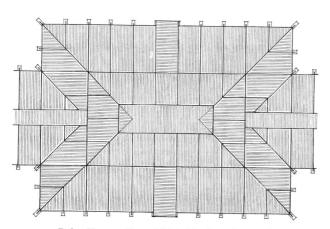

Palm House, Kew, 1844-48, elevation and
plan of central transept

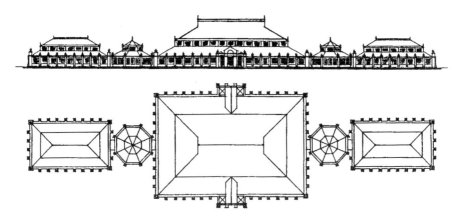

Temperate House, Kew Gardens

Work on the Temperate House at Kew started in 1860. On 28th March 1859 Decimus Burton wrote to Sir William Hooker to the effect that he had been working on the design, wood being adopted for the sashes instead of iron (5). The wings are linked to the main building by octagonal vestibules. About double the size of the Palm House, the Temperate House is claimed to be the world's largest surviving Victorian glass structure, and it is a very handsome one.

Other works by Burton at Kew are Museum No.1, the Campanile, and the Main Entrance Gates to Kew Green. The Royal Botanic Gardens at Kew were included in the Government's list of potential World Heritage Sites, published in 1999(6), and were the subject of the UK's 2002 nomination to UNESCO for World Heritage Status.

Palmette border, based on ironwork at the Palm House, Kew

CHAPTER 9

THE CONSUMMATE PROFESSIONAL

The second quarter of the 19th century was a period when the architectural profession was endeavouring to organise itself on a proper basis. First tentative steps in this direction had been taken towards the end of the 18th century, with the formation of the Architects' Club and the Surveyors' Club. However, these were primarily social and dining clubs and a far cry from any body that would today be recognized as resembling a professional association. Nevertheless, by the 1830s serious efforts were being made to unite the profession, and in 1834 the Institute was born, with Decimus Burton as an original Fellow (1). The Institute received its Royal Charter of incorporation in 1837 and Burton served as its Vice-President in 1839.

From around 1824 Burton was practising in London's Regent Street but, in about 1827, he took a lease from the Crown on land in Spring Gardens. There he built nos. 10, 12 and 14, which he occupied as a town house and London office for many years. The buildings no longer exist, but elevations of them appear in the former LCC's Survey of London Vol. XX (2). They were characteristic London houses in the late Georgian tradition, with a rusticated ground storey and three upper floors. Interestingly, views of the interior have been preserved in Hastings Museum and show casts of architectural details which probably doubled as a reference collection and as a means of impressing clients with the scholarship of his work.

In Tunbridge Wells, Burton had an office at No.10 Calverley Parade (3), where the Civic Centre now stands. The census for 1851 gives the occupants of the property as James Dean, Architect's Clerk, and his wife Mary Ann. Burton must have had a number of Clerks during the course of his long architectural career, and Henry Sandall and William Selway are names of former Clerks specifically mentioned in his will.

A particular issue exercising the minds of architects in the 1820s concerned the form of agreement for building work.

One method of proceeding which was under discussion at that time was that of "contracts in gross", whereby works were performed for a fixed sum.

The other way was that adopted by the Office of Works, which was to contract on terms of "measure and prices".

The attraction of work being done for a fixed sum was obvious, but the attendant risks of "contracts in gross" were seen as making badly executed or fraudulent work more likely and more difficult to detect. Burton, along with Sir Robert Smirke and Sir Jeffry Wyatville, favoured the official and potentially safer course of "measure and prices" (4).

On the matter of fees charged to a private client, and the professional services provided for those fees, Burton set out his position clearly in a letter of 29th August 1828, which survives at the Centre for Kentish Studies and concerns "The Grove" at Penshurst.

The "customary remuneration for Architects", writes Burton, is five per cent on the cost of a building for preparing the design, working drawings and specification, superintending of the work and settling the account. The fee would be reduced to two and a half per cent where no superintendence or settling of accounts is required, and travelling expenses are charged for country work. Four visits he envisages as sufficient during the progress of the works, if a Clerk of Works is employed, a course which he strongly advises and requests. "There is", he concludes, "great advantage in clear explanations in all matter of business, and friendships are strengthened rather than weakened by following this course".

Remuneration for the office of Architect to the Zoological Society of London was necessarily on a different basis. There, Burton expressed his willingness to act as the Society's Architect for an annual salary of £150, on the understanding that his duties would be to provide designs, working drawings and superintendence of new building works or laying out of the gardens with "frequent attendance as hitherto". Burton added the proviso that if "buildings or works of magnitude, such as the museum etc." were to be required, then he would be satisfied with an extra £150 per annum during the execution of such works, which "would not more than pay the actual cost of the drawings that would be required" (5).

London Zoo in the 1830s, from a series of views by James Hakewill.
(The tent-shaped Macaw cage, later the Raven Cage, is on the right of the picture.)

In accepting Burton's terms, the Council of the Society asked that a report be provided on the first Wednesday of each month setting out the works ordered, in hand, and completed since the preceding report. Also, the Council allowed Burton to give directions for works up to £5, above which figure previous consent would be needed. As a matter of interest, for comparative purposes, a kangaroo purchased by the Society at that time cost £6.

Burton was elected a Fellow of the Royal Society in 1832 and, in its proceedings following his death the Society commented upon Burton's "thoroughly gentlemanly conduct in all his business arrangements", adding: "In no instance was Mr. Burton ever suspected of sacrificing the interest of a client for his own glorification, or for the indulgence of his own individual fancies. Having placed at his client's disposal all the resources of his long experience, and sound practical sense and good taste, he set loyally to carry out the wishes of his employer with an amount of self-negation rare in the profession" (6). A fitting tribute to a consummate professional.

CHAPTER 10

BURTON'S LEGACY

Decimus Burton retired from practice in 1869 (1) and spent his seventies partly at Gloucester Gardens, near Hyde Park in London, and partly at "St.Leonards Lodge", off Maze Hill in St.Leonards, adjoining "The Uplands" and "The Lawn" development which he designed. St.Leonards, of course, was the creation of his father, James. The practice was continued for a while by Decimus's nephew and pupil Henry Marley Burton, the son of his brother William (2). Henry Marley Burton had become an Associate of the RIBA in 1860, proposed by Decimus Burton, Sir James Pennethorne and Sydney Smirke (3).

A lifelong bachelor, Decimus Burton died on 14th December 1881 at his London home, and he is buried at Kensal Green Cemetery. It was his wish that he be buried there if he died in London, although he is also commemorated on the pyramid-topped family vault at St.Leonards. It was his wish, too, that his funeral should be "plain and simple" (4), and "strictly private and economical".

His legacies, in the literal sense of articles given by will, shed just a little more light on Decimus Burton, the man, in terms of his possessions, his family and his staff. Among his possessions was an oil painting of

St.John, copied by Sir Joshua Reynolds from a work by Raphael; a model of the Temple on the Ilissus at Athens; a statuette of an Angel, after Thorwaldsen; framed drawings of a Royal Palace by Joseph Gandy ARA (1771-1843), once described as an "English Piranesi"; a bronze lamp suspended from a snake's mouth; and, of course, casts and architectural books.

Burton family vault at St. Leonards-on-Sea

There were bequests to the RIBA; to Charing Cross Hospital; and to his many relations, including his nieces Emily and Helen Wood, daughters of his sister Jane. To them he left a life interest in St.Leonards Lodge. Nor did he forget his servants, and to each that had been in his service for a year, he left a year's wages.

With regard to his wider architectural legacy, from a national perspective his most obvious memorials will

St. Leonards Lodge, Decimus Burton's villa at Maze Hill, St. Leonards-on-Sea.

be the neo-classical tours de force, including the Wellington Arch and the Athenaeum Club, together with the great glass-houses that formed part of the UK's case for World Heritage Site status at Kew.

In and around Tunbridge Wells, however, it is his picturesque and planning work that is of especial importance. In his book on the architect Norman Shaw, the architectural historian Professor Andrew Saint touched upon the artistic movement in the area around Penshurst, identifying "the architectural connections of the Penshurst set" (5) as Salvin, Burton and Devey. The clients for Burton's "The Grove" knew the Devey family well (6). Thus it is by no means fanciful to suggest that Burton's early contributions, such as "The Grove", Burrswood and Bentham Hill could well have had a direct influence upon Voysey's master George Devey and, indirectly upon the wider Arts and Crafts movement.

As for Burton's pupils, mention has already been made of Henry Currey, for his work at Eastbourne, and E.J. May, for his work at Bedford Park. To the list can be added George Mair, who was articled to Burton in 1826, and later acted for Nash's friend and business associate, George Ward, on Northwood House at Cowes on the Isle of Wight (7). Other pupils include John Crake in 1828 (8) and Arthur

William Hakewill. A.W. Hakewill was the author of an architectural pamphlet favouring a classical style, rather than a gothic one, for the new Houses of Parliament (9). Not surprisingly this provoked a sharp response from A.W.N. Pugin.

Importantly in Tunbridge Wells, the major figure of William Willicombe, although not an architectural pupil as such, worked with Burton on the early development of the Calverley Estate and Willicombe's later developments in Lansdowne Road, Calverley Park Gardens and elsewhere clearly reflect the influence of the association.

In Tunbridge Wells, Burton's legacy is immeasurable. Not only does this comprise the remarkable sequence of villas in their landscape setting of Calverley Park, the sweep of Calverley Park Crescent, the landmark of Trinity, and the remaining buildings of the "new town", but other land-owners took up the park theme. To the east, Camden Park was laid out on the Camden Estate, it is said with help from Burton. To the west, Nevill Park and Hungershall Park were laid out on the Abergavenny Estate, and by the end of the 19th century Tunbridge Wells was ringed with a series of "parks" that have given to the historic spa town the open-textured and sylvan character that has remained a feature to this day.

As long ago as 1927, an article in the Architect's Journal on Burton's Tunbridge Wells, summed up Burton the man, and his legacy in Tunbridge Wells. A contemporary obituary notice, it said, spoke of him as a straightforward, high-principled and cultured man. "No architect", it went on, "was better known, and none was better respected, for he was amiable, considerate, and gentle to all".

Burton, it was observed, "found Tunbridge Wells but little more than a village and he made it a considerable town" (9).

Gothick border based on the former conservatory at Burrswood

NOTES AND REFERENCES

The Introduction
1. Society of Antiquaries Minute Book, Vol. XXXV, p.432, 19.6.1828
2. Christopher Hussey, Country Life 8.5.1969, p.1166

Chapter 1
1. Baines, J.M. *Burton's St.Leonards*, 1956, p.58
2. Amsinck, P. *Tunbridge Wells* 1810, p.93
3. Letter, dated 19.3.1869 from Wyatt Papworth to J.P. Seddon in RIBA Drawings Collection
4. Hutchinson, S.C. *The Royal Academy Schools 1768-1830*, Walpole Society Vol.38, p.127
5. Watkin, D. *Sir John Soane*, Enlightenment thought and the Royal Academy Lectures, 1996, p.574
6. Op.cit., p.588
7. V and A Gallery, 118c
8. Newman, J. *Gwent/Monmouthshire: The Buildings of Wales*, 2000, p.110
9. Monkhouse, C. *Fleetwood, Lancashire – I:* Country Life, Vol CLVIII No.4072 17.7.1975, p.126
10. *English Letters A-H, 1858-61,* Vol XXIX No.143, Letter to Sir William Hooker, 4.4.1859
11. Op.cit., No.152, Letter of 8.8.1860

Chapter 2
1. Ann Saunders *The Regent's Park Villas*, p.8.
2. Colvin, H. *Biographical Dictionary of Architects*, p.194
3. *Survey of London*, Vol XXXIX, p.287
4. *The Wellington Arch*, English Heritage, p.7
5. CKS. U2737. Box 16 Crown lease to Ward of 10.12.1823 and Indenture Ward/James Burton 3.3.1825
6. Based upon Sir Bernard Burke's *Landed Gentry of Great Britain 1906*, p.1749
7. J. and J.B. Burke, *Dictionary of Landed Gentry*, Vol.II M-Z, 1847, p.1516
8. The Builder, 24.12.1881, p.780
9. CKS. U2737. Box 16. Indenture 26.4.1836
10. CKS. U2737. Box 16. Covenant 31.5.1834
11. The Tunbridge Wells Visitor, Vol.4, No.17, 25.3.1834, p.275
12. The Architects' Compendium, 1914, Section L, pp.570& 571

Chapter 3
1. Honour, H. *The Regent's Park Colosseum* Country Life Vol.CXIII, 2.1.1953, p.22
2. Summerson, Sir John, *Architecture in Britain 1530-1830*, p.505

Chapter 4
1. The Builder, 24.12.1881, p.780
2. CKS. U55 T531, 533
3. Map of the estate, Tunbridge Wells Museum
4. CKS. U55 T531, 533
5. Phippen, J. *Colbran's New Guide for Tunbridge Wells* (second edition) 1844, p.47
6. Britton, J. *Descriptive sketches of Tunbridge Wells and the Calverley Estate*, 1832, p.44
7. Ibid. p.54
8. *Colbran's Handbook and Dictionary for Tunbridge Wells*, 1847, p.121
9. CKS, Indenture 26.4.1836, second schedule of tenancies
10. Hitchcock, H.R. *Early Victorian Architecture in Britain*, Vol.I, p.449
11. Ibid.
12. *Auction Sales 1945-8*, Vol. 15, No.53
13. 1841 Census Return
14. The Tunbridge Wells Visitor, Vol.2, No.16, 19.4.1834, p.246
15. Ibid.
16. The Tunbridge Wells Visitor, Vol.3 No.17, 18.10.1834, p.254
17. Ibid
18. Ibid, p.255
19. *Colbran's New Guide for Tunbridge Wells*, 1839, p.56
20. The Tunbridge Wells Visitor, Vol.2, No.16, 19.4.1834, p.247
21. *Colbran's New Guide for Tunbridge Wells*, 1839, p.56
22. Ibid p.54
23. The Tunbridge Wells Visitor, Vol.3, No.14, 4.10.1834, p.209
23. Ibid, Vol.4, No.15, 11.4.1835, p.258.

Chapter 5
1. Plan of Royal Botanic Society garden referred to in Burton and Marnock's Report of July 1840 in Hastings Museum
2. *Colbran's New Guide for Tunbridge Wells, 1840*, p.33
3. Ibid.
4. Britton, J. *Descriptive Sketches of Tunbridge Wells and the Calverley Estate*, 1832, p.55
5. Ibid.
6. Greenwood, C. *An Epitome of County History. Vol. I, Kent, 1838*, p.117

7. Ernest, J. *This House named Burrwood*, 1989, p.16
8. Greenwood, C. p.125
9. CKS, U1050
10. Zoological Society, Minutes of Council, Vol.I 5th May 1826-4th August 1830, pp.1, 3, 5 and 6.
11. Ibid, P.414
12. Guillery, P. *The Buildings of London Zoo*, RCHME, 1993, p.2
13. Weatherhead, G.H., *An Account of the Beulah Saline Spa at Norwood, Surrey,* 1832, pp.6 and 7
14. Ford, J. and J. *Images of Brighton*, 1981, p.123.

Chapter 6

1. Graves, A. *The Royal Academy of Arts Exhibitors 1769-1904*, 1989, p.358
2. Pugin, A.C., *Specimens of Gothic Architecture*, Vols.1 and 2, 1821 and 1823.
3. John Bull, Vol.IX, No.458, 20.9.1829, p.303.
4. *Clifford's Visitor's Guide to Tunbridge Wells, 1853*, p.31.
5. Colbran's *New Guide for Tunbridge Wells, 1839*, p.93.
6. Barton, M. *Tunbridge Wells*, 1937, pp.322/323
7. Port, M.H. *Six Hundred New Churches, The Church Building Commission 1818-1856*, 1961, p.146.
8. Clark, K. *The Gothic Revival*, 1928, p.119.
9. Original South elevation CKS, U1350, initialled DB and dated October 1830.
10. Eastbourne Civic Society, *Eight Town Walks in Eastbourne*, 1981, p.49
11. Elleray, D. *The Victorian Churches of Sussex*, 1981, p.61.
12. Drewe, F. *Ticehurst, Stonegate and Flimwell*, 1991, p.85
13. CKS, Minutes of Trustees of KCM, 23.4.1829, 7/20/30.5.1929.
14. Esdaile, Mrs E., *Temple Church Monuments*, 1933, p.44.

Chapter 7

1. Monkhouse, C., *"A New Lanark by the sea"* Country Life, Vol.CLVIII, No.4072, 17.7.1975, p.126.
2. Dale, A., *Fashionable Brighton 1820-1860*, 1947, p.151.
3. Eastbourne Civic Society, *Eight Town Walks in Eastbourne*, 1981, p.5.
4. Williamson, E., Riches, A., Higgs, M., *Glasgow*, 1990, pp.46 and 308.
5. Newman, J., *North East and East Kent* 1969, p.314.
6. Pevsner, N. and Lloyd, D., *Hampshire*, 1967, p.117.

Chapter 8
1. Gloag, J., *Mr Loudon's England*, 1970, p.45.
2. Hussey, C., *Grimston Park*, Country Life 87, 16.3.1940, p.280.
3. Kew Archives, Works 32, Palm House.
4. Cherry, B. and Pevsner, N., *London 2 : South* 1983, p.510.
5. Kew Archives, *English Letters A-H, 1858-61*, Vol. XXIX, No.142.
6. DCMS, UK *Tentative List of World Heritage Sites*, 1999, pp.17 and 37-40.

Chapter 9
1. British Architectural Library, *Directory of British Architects 1834-1900*, 1993, p.142.
2. LCC, *Survey of London*, Vol.XX, 1940 (Trafalgar Square and Neighbourhood), plate 48.
3. *Colbran's Handbook and Directory for Tunbridge Wells, 1847*, p.114.
4. *History of the King's Works*, Vol.VI, 1782-1851, 1973, pp.161-2.
5. Zoological Society, Minutes of Council Vol. I, 2.6.1830, pp.414 and 415.
6. Proceedings of the Royal Society Vol. XXXIV, 1883, p.ix.

Chapter 10
1. Proceedings of the Royal Society, Vol.XXXIV, 1883, p.x.
2. Relationship stated in Decimus Burton's Will dated 30.6.1870.
3. *Directory of British Architects 1834-1900*, RIBA, 1993, p.143.
4. Will of Decimus Burton, dated 30.6.1870.
5. Saint, A., *Richard Norman Shaw*, 1976, pp.25/26.
6. Ibid. pp.442/3.
7. The Builder obit., Vol.57, 1889, p.104.
8. The Builder obit., Vol.18, 1960, p.6
9. Hakewill, A.W., *Thoughts upon the Style of Architecture to be adopted in rebuilding the Houses of Parliament*, 1835.
10. McRae, J.F., *Burton's Tunbridge Wells*, Architects Journal, 16.2.1927, pp.249/50.

Calverley Park, Tunbridge Wells

SHORT BIBLIOGRAPHY

Baines, J. Manwaring : *Burton's St.Leonards*, Hastings Museum, 1956

Bohan, Peter J : *Decimus Burton*, Macmillan, Encyclopedia of Architects, Vol.1, 1982

Brindle, Dr. Steven, and David Robinson : *The Wellington Arch and The Marble Arch*, English Heritage, 2001

Britton, John : *Descriptive Sketches of Tunbridge Wells and the Calverley Estate*, 1832

Burnett, G.W : Decimus Burton entry in the *Dictionary of National Biography*, 1973

Chalkin, C.W : *Estate Development and the beginnings of modern Tunbridge Wells, 1800-40* Archael.Cant. Vol.100, 1983

Colvin, Howard : *A Biographical Dictionary of British Architects 1600-1840* (Third Edition), 1995

Crook, J.M. and Port, M.H., *The History of the King's Works*, Vol.VI, 1782-1851, 1973

Farthing, Roger : *Royal Tunbridge Wells – A Pictorial History*, 1990

Graves, Algernon : *The Royal Academy Exhibitors 1769-1904*, Royal Academy of Arts, 1989

Hussey, Christopher : *Calverley Park, Tunbridge Wells* Country Life, 1st and 8th May 1979

Jones, Ronald P : *The Life and Work of Decimus Burton*, Architectural Review xvii, 1905

London County Council : *Survey of London Vol. XX Trafalgar Square and Neighbourhood*, 1940

Miller, Philip : *Decimus Burton 1800-1881*. Exhibition Guide, The Building Centre Trust, 1981

Newman, John : *West Kent and the Weald*. The Buildings of England series, 1976

Phippen, James : *Colbran's New Guide for Tunbridge Wells, 1840*

Reilly, Sir Paul *: An Introduction to Regency Architecture,* 1948

Royal Institute of British Architects : *Catalogue of the Drawings Collection, 1972*

Saunders, Ann : *The Regent's Park Villas,* Bedford College, 1981

Savidge, Alan : *Royal Tunbridge Wells,* 1975

Summerson, Sir John : *Architecture in Britain 1530-1830* (Sixth edition), 1977

Summerson, Sir John : *The Life and Work of John Nash, Architect,* 1980

Tunbridge Wells Museum and Art Gallery : *Decimus Burton Centenary Exhibition,* Catalogue 1981

Whitbourn, Dr Philip : *A look around Trinity.* Trinity Theatre and Arts Association, 1978

Williams, Guy : *Augustus Pugin versus Decimus Burton. A Victorian Architectural Duel,* 1990

South Villa, Regent's Park. Built 1818-19, demolished in 1930

INDEX

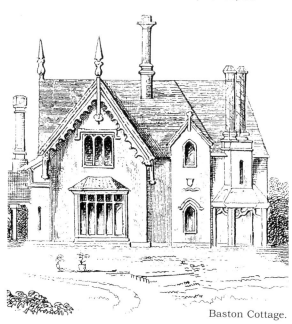

Baston Cottage.